THE WOMEN'S INSTITUTE

Susan Cohen

SHIRE PUBLICATIONS

Published in Great Britain in 2011 by Shire Publications Ltd, Midland House, West Way, Botley, Oxford OX2 0PH, United Kingdom.

44-02 23rd Street, Suite 219, Long Island City, NY 11101, USA.

E-mail: shire@shirebooks.co.uk   www.shirebooks.co.uk

A CIP catalogue record for this book is available from the British Library.

Shire Library no. 643.   ISBN-13: 978 0 74781 046 9

Susan Cohen has asserted her right under the Copyright, Designs and Patents Act, 1988, to be identified as the author of this book.

Designed by Tony Truscott Designs, Sussex, UK and typeset in Perpetua and Gill Sans.
Printed in China through Worldprint Ltd.

11 12 13 14 15   10 9 8 7 6 5 4 3 2 1

COVER IMAGE
1941: in one day alone, the WI in Brimpton, Berkshire, made as much as 217 pounds of jam from local fruit.

TITLE PAGE IMAGE
WI members at a fruit-bottling demonstration at Newtown County Girls' School, Powys, 24 August 1940.

CONTENTS PAGE IMAGE
Members of the Shipston on Stour WI Dramatic Society performing *Aladdin* in 1929.

ACKNOWLEDGEMENTS
My thanks to Debbie Allen, Irene Beadsworth, Colin Boylett, Bill Brown, Andy Bush, Michael Cadwell, Rosalie Cole, Chris Copp, Tim Eades, Cedric Ellis, Alison Ferguson, Rog Frost, Ruth Gill, Michael Greatorex, Peter Greener, Christine Hammond, Linda Haywood, Phyllis Higton, Mike Hitchins, Peter Leigh, Nigel Lutt, Tony Mansell, Ivor Martin, Jenny Murray, Sylvia Reed, Hugh Roberts, Keith Roberts, Kathleen Sargent, Pauline Smeed, Jane Smith, Mrs Margaret Smith, Maureen Spinks, Gary Strutt, Ann Walker, Angela Watkins, Laura Wigg-Bailey and Brian Wright for their generous help in locating and providing images. I would also like to thank the innumerable local history societies, heritage groups and archives, too numerous to mention individually, who generously provided information about their Women's Institutes.

Illustrations are produced by courtesy of:

Alstonefield Local History Society, p. 19; Anglesey Library, p. 50; Ashwell Museum, pp. 15, 16, 40, 48, 59; Badsey WI, p. 46; Bangor University Archives, pp. 6 and 7; Barford WI, p. 31; Barmouth WI, p. 29; Bedfordshire and Luton Archives, p. 14; Bedfordshire and Luton Archives (*Bedfordshire Times*), pp. 23, 37, 39, 53, 57 ; Bedfordshire and Luton Archives (Bedfordshire Federation of Women's Institutes) pp. 11, 22, 23, 24, 50, 53; Bishopthorpe Community Archive / Mrs Margaret Smith, p. 43; Bramley WI Lite, p. 62; Michael Cadwell, p. 14; Colton History Society, p. 47; Cottingham History, p. 49; Crafty Green Village Hall Committee, p. 25; Dales Countryside Museum, pp. 17, 28; Dunbar and District History Society, p. 30; Etchingham WI, p. 34; Getty Images, pp. 59, 61; Gloucestershire Archives, p. 8; Phyllis Higton, p. 52 (top); Imperial War Museum, pp. 35, 36; Kirkby Malzeard WI, p. 60; Market Lavington Museum, pp. 52, 55; Milton Malsor WI, p. 57; Museum of English Rural Life, Reading, pp. 18, 21, 25; National Library of Wales, pp. 1, 26, 28, 42, 44, 46, 47; National Portrait Gallery, London, p. 8; Pattingham Local History & Civic Society, p. 31; Mrs Kathleen Sargent, pp. 32, 58; Shetland Museum and Archives, p. 23; Somerset County Federation of Women's Institutes, p. 12; Staffordshire Arts and Museum Service, p. 54; Gary Strutt, p. 15; SWRI, Longniddry Branch, pp. 9, 10; Dora Tack and Hilton WI, p. 49; Topfoto, p. 61; Uttoxeter Town Council, p. 18; Warwickshire County Record Office, p. 2; Winteringham WI, p. 16; Brian Wright, p. 51.

"Aladdin" - Shipston W.I.D.S. 1929 5.

CONTENTS

with HAMPSHIRE SUPPLEMENT—2½d.

HOME AND COUNTRY

THE JOURNAL OF THE WOMEN'S INSTITUTES

Vol. XV.
No. 10

OCT.
1933

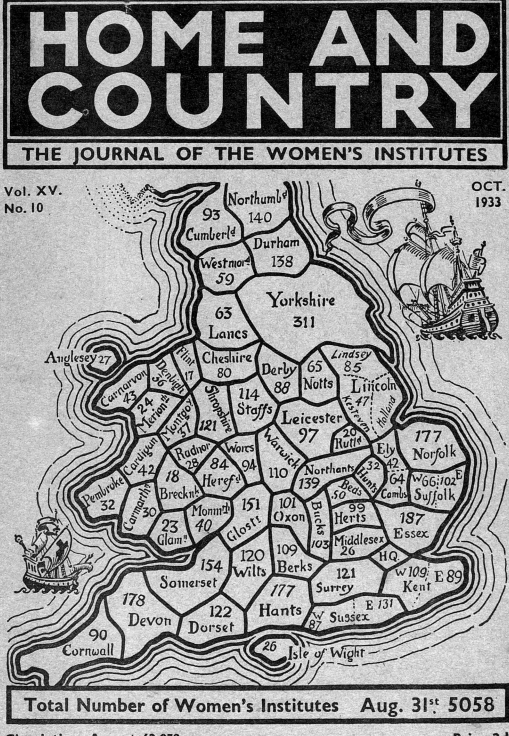

Northumb⁴ 140
93 Cumberld
Durham 138
Westmor⁴ 59
63 Lancs
Yorkshire 311
Anglesey 27
Flint 17
Cheshire 80
Derby 88
65 Notts
Lindsey 85
Carnarvon 43
Denbigh 36
24 Merion⁴
Shropshire
114 Staffs
Lincoln
Kesteven 47
Holland
Montgoy 37
121
Radnor 28
Worcs 94
Leicester 97
20 Rutld
Ely 42
177 Norfolk
Cardigan 42
18 Hereford
84
Warwick 110
Northants 139
32 Hunts
64 Cambs
W 66 102 E Suffolk
Pembroke 32
Carmarthen 30
Brecknⁱᵏ
Monm⁴ʰ 40
151 Glosʳ
101 Oxon
Bucks
Beds 50
99 Herts
187 Essex
23 Glamᵗⁿ
120 Wilts
109 Berks
Middlesex 26
H.Q.
154 Somerset
121 Surrey
W 109 Kent E 89
178 Devon
122 Dorset
177 Hants
W 87 E 131 Sussex
90 Cornwall
26 Isle of Wight

Total Number of Women's Institutes   Aug. 31ˢᵗ 5058

Circulation August 63,958   Price 2d.

INTRODUCTION

THE WOMEN'S INSTITUTE (WI) is so much a part of the fabric of British society that it is hard to imagine a time when it did not exist. Its inception is, indeed, beyond living memory, for the first WI opened its doors to a small group of womenfolk in the village of Llanfair PG, Anglesey in 1915. The idea owed much to Mrs Madge Watt, whose experience of the WI in Canada, and of the benefits it brought to rural women and wider society, encouraged her to pressure people with influence in Britain to at least try the idea here. There was no certainty that this venture would succeed, but the sceptics were soon proved wrong, for the organisation grew apace to become, in the first decade of the twenty-first century, the country's largest voluntary women's organisation. The WI now boasts a membership of some 205,000 women spread across 6,500 local groups in Britain, Wales and the Islands, and the women, whose ages range from eighteen to eighty plus, come from all walks of life, with working women equal in status to those of the royal family who belong. They meet, as they have always done (except during exceptional times) once a month, to socialise, be educated and entertained, and to expand their horizons in all sorts of ways, giving thousands of women a new kind of freedom and independence. The ethos of the WI has always been to inspire women, to teach them new skills and to generally improve the quality of their lives and of those around them: nowhere was this better demonstrated than in the late 1990s, when the bold ladies of Rylstone WI in Yorkshire posed for their nearly-nude calendar to raise money for leukaemia research. This, and the spin-off, *Calendar Girls*, the film and stage show, certainly challenged the popular image of the WI as being the province of elderly ladies in village communities – although the old idea still lingered, immortalised in the comedy drama series, 'Jam and Jerusalem', in 2006. But change is on the way, for as rural communities and village WIs diminish there is a growing generation of enthusiastic younger women members setting up groups in the inner cities where they now live and work. They are keen to leave their own mark on society and be remembered for more than making jam and singing 'Jerusalem'.

Opposite:
Front cover of
Home and Country,
October 1933,
showing the
spread of WIs.

5

General Meetings.

An open meeting was held at Craig on Sep. 11th 1915 when it was decided to form a branch of the Women's Institutes. The following Committee was elected.

President.   The Honble Mrs Stapleton-Cott...
Vice President & Treasurer   Mrs W. E. Jones Craig
Hon. Secretary   Mrs Wilson Bryn.

Committee

Mrs Williams   Trenarfon +
  „ Morris Jones   Ty Coch + present
  „ Edwards   Sydeln Jedog +
  „ Jones   Bron Llwyn
Miss B. Pritchard   Menai House
      Watts   Aberbraint. +
Miss Roberts   Post Office. dead

Sep. 16th At this meeting Mr Watt of the W. I.
           Canada, now with the A. O. S. explained
           the object of the movement. The following
           resolutions were put to the meeting and carrie...

I Prop. by Mrs Cotton sec: by Miss Roberts
That we form a W. I. in Llanfairpwll, affiliated
     to the A. O. S.

I Prop: by Mrs Cotton sec: by Mrs W. E Jones
That it be called the "Llanfairpwll Women's
Institute.

ORIGINS OF THE INSTITUTE

What is a Women's Institute? A group of women banded together to help their country and themselves.

Federation of Women's Institutes.

The inspiration for the Women's Institute (WI), the largest women's voluntary organisation in Britain, came from Canada, where the first WI was set up by Mrs Adelaide Hoodless and Mr Erland Lee at Stoney Creek, in 1897. Their mission was to harness the skills of country women, encourage them to play a more active role in village life and give them new opportunities to share activities. Britain was slow to follow and it was only after Mrs Alfred Watt, a pioneering Canadian WI member, moved to Britain in 1913 that progress was made. She immediately recognised the benefits a similar organisation could have for the country's women, and provided the impetus for the establishment of the movement in Britain. Mrs Watt was no shrinking violet, and having sat through to the very end of an Agricultural Organisation Society (AOS) conference in London in February 1915, she put down her knitting and boldly recounted the story of the WI movement in Canada and of their co-operative ideals. The AOS secretary, Mr Nugent Harris, was so enthused by what he heard that by July 1915 he had persuaded his fellow members to try the WI idea, and gave Mrs Watt three months in which to see if she could make it work.

Opposite and below: The front cover and title page from the first Llanfair Women's Institute Minute Book, 1915.

And work it certainly did, for by September 1915, the first WI of England and Wales was established in the small Anglesey village of Llanfair, marking the start of a great journey. Against the odds – the village women were suspicious and reluctant to accept this novel, even radical, concept – this initial venture was soon copied on the Welsh mainland in Cefn and Trefnant, Denbighshire. In England, Mrs Watt was personally responsible for the establishment of the first two WIs at Singleton and East Dean in Sussex and Wallisdown, Dorset.

First day cover celebrating the sixtieth anniversary of Llanfair WI, 1975.

DIAMOND JUBILEE W.I.
11 SEPT 1975
LLANFAIRPWLLGWYNGYLL—
GOGERYCHWYRNDROBWLL—
LLANDYSILICGOGOGOCH,
GWYNEDD

Mrs. Shellard ~ President
Hillesley & District W.I.,
Mitre Cottage, Wortley Rd.,
Wotton-under-Edge, Glos.

FIRST DAY COVER

pwllgwyngyllgogerychwyrndrobwllllandysiliogogogoch

More groups were opened during 1916 in villages across the country, and, buoyed by success, Mrs Watt's temporary engagement was extended and a WI sub-committee was formed to help in the creation and organisation of the new branches. But a chairman was needed and in an inspirational move, thirty-three-year-old Lady Gertrude Denman, a campaigner for women's suffrage, and a sound, intelligent

Gertrude Mary Denman (née Pearson), 21 March 1918. Lady Denman was thirty-three years old when she was appointed to run the WI.

FOR HOME AND COUNTRY.

Creuncsli — Women's Institute.

MEMBERSHIP CARD. 1916.

"To do all the good we can, in every way we can, to all the people we can ; and above all to study household good in any line of work which makes for the betterment of our home, the advancement of our people, and the good of our country."

I, whose name is subscribed hereto, being desirous of becoming a member of The ......Creuncsli......
......Women's Institute, of ....do agree to pay to the Treasurer of the said Institute the sum of ......£......yearly while I continue a member of the said Institute ; and I further agree to conform to and abide by the rules and bye-laws of the said Institute and all rules and regulations duly made for the government and management of Women's Institutes in England and Wales.

Member's Name   Mrs C. A. Hadow

    Lose Ladye Creuncsli
        & Trotman Hon. Secretary.

July 7-1916

Grace Hadow's membership card.

businesswoman with first-hand experience of rural life and the needs of the community, was appointed. Miss Grace Hadow, another suffrage campaigner and tutor at Lady Margaret Hall, Oxford, was elected as vice-chairman, creating a partnership that lasted over twenty years. A set of model rules and regulations, intended to safeguard the democratic, non-sectarian and non-party-political nature of the organisation, was established, and these ideals still endure in the twenty-first century. Scotland and Northern Ireland remained independent of the English organisation, forming their own WIs, with the first Scottish Women's Rural Institute (SWRI) set up in Longniddry, East Lothian, on 26 June 1917. Getting the 'Rurals' going was challenging, as Catherine Blair, the driving force behind the foundation of the SWRI, recalled in June 1938: 'The women of East Lothian hardly left the cottar house in the course of a year. Their one holiday and their one opportunity of

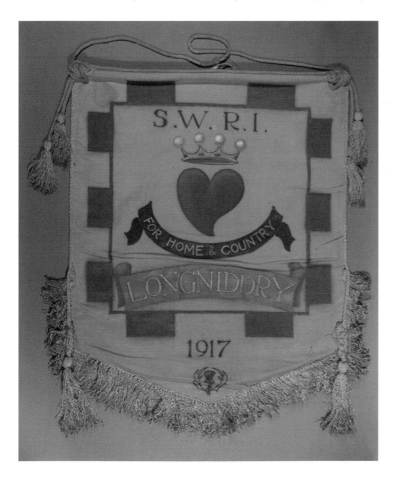

Catherine Blair's banner for the Longniddry Institute. The reverse has the phrase 'Deeds Not Words', the motto of more active members of the suffrage campaign.

Catherine Blair (left) and her assistant, Betty Wight, each holding a Toby jug made in Blair's Mak'Merry Pottery in the town of MacMerry, near Gladsmuir, East Lothian, 1920s.

meeting their friends was Haddington Fair Day.' To promote the idea, she even went to two other counties to demonstrate 'How to Cut up a Pig', aided by 'the minister's man in his Sunday suit on one occasion, and a handsome farmer in a large overall on another.'

The impetus for WIs continued unabated, increasing from 40 to 199 during 1917, even though not everyone was convinced that the venture would succeed. Most had greater faith than South Cerney in Gloucestershire, who kept very sketchy minutes in the early days, and in September 1917 the sixteen WIs in East and West Sussex united forces to become the Sussex Women's Institute Conference, so forming the first County Federation (CF) who oversaw and organised the WIs within their boundary. But at the same time, a financial crisis loomed, when the AOS informed the WIs that they could no longer divert any money – which came mostly from Government – to the venture. Inez Jenkins recounts how Lady Denman was determined to 'safeguard the democratic and independent character of the Institute,' and a happy compromise was reached when Mr Prothero, the President of the Board of Agriculture, agreed that his organisation would fund the establishment of new WIs, but after that they would be left to self-govern. A separate organisation, as envisaged by Lady Denman, was to undertake this role, and this was how the National Federation of Women's Institutes (NF) came to be formed on 16 October 1917. Representatives from sixty of the existing 137 WIs met in Central Hall, Westminster, and agreed the acceptance of a constitution and rules. A Central Committee of Management was adopted, Lady Denman was elected Chair, and besides the ten elected members, representatives were appointed from various government departments that provided financial support or had similar interests to the newly formed NF. Before long, all WIs and CFs became affiliated to this unifying body.

The year 1918 proved to be so busy that the paid organisers found it impossible to cope with the demand for new WIs. The solution reached was to appoint Voluntary County Organisers (VCOs) who attended the newly established VCO training school, with funds for this enterprise coming from yet another 'first', the National Craft Exhibition, held at Caxton Hall, London in October 1917. This exhibition, like the one that followed in 1920, proved to be a popular and financial success, with sales of goods and produce showing an excellent profit.

Bedfordshire
Federation display
of handicrafts at
the County Show,
1951.

Launching the WI's own journal in March 1919, *Home and Country*, with the Institute's motto as its title, was a brave move, for although the Executive Committee were convinced that this would be an ideal way of uniting WI members, they really had no idea what the demand would be. They need not have worried for, within a year, the little eight-page magazine had, according to Inez Jenkins, doubled in size and almost trebled in circulation. By 1927, just twelve years after the first WI had opened, 50,000 copies of *Home and Country* were distributed to WI members across the organisation. The content of the early magazine was a mix of 'helpful household hints', short stories, homilies and recipes, to say nothing of the adverts for everything from Carr's Water Biscuits and Ovaltine to embroidery thread, but it soon became a

An advertisement
from *Home and
Country*, July 1921,
offering the
expertise of
Mrs D. E. Bertram
on matters of
interest to
Institute members.

forum for highly qualified professionals to pass on guidance, such as the series of articles on 'Design in Country Things' contributed by Professor W. R. Lethaby, the founding principal of the Central School of Arts and Crafts. The content and style of the magazine was replicated when the SWRI's own magazine *Scottish Home and Country* was founded in 1924, while in Northern Ireland, what started as a one-penny news sheet in 1935, developed into a regular magazine, the *Ulster Countrywoman*.

Mrs. D. E. BERTRAM,

62E, NEVERN SQUARE, LONDON, S.W.5.

Will be in TYNEMOUTH, NORTHUMBERLAND, for end of August and part of September and is willing to lecture on :—

**Domestic Economy.
A Journey Round the World.
Fuel Saving and Fuel Making.
Women and Citizenship.**

FEE—£1 1s. and travelling expenses or if a tour were arranged of three or more Institutes they could share travelling expenses and the fee per lecture would be 17s. 6d. Please book early.

THE EARLY WIS

The success of an institute must depend on the inclusion of women of all ranks in its scope. Their aim of mutual help and combined effort can only be achieved by a better understanding of each other's needs and interests and the points of view from which these are regarded.

Women's Institutes and their part in the reconstruction of rural life, published by NF in 1917.

The remarkable thing about the new WIs was that they really did cater for women from every walk of life. Domestic staff shared the tea table and platform with the grand ladies who employed them, and all rubbed shoulders with farmers' and vicars' wives, shop assistants and teachers. Many, like Edith Rigby, a founder member and first President of Hutton and Howick WI, which was the first institute to be formed in Lancashire in 1918, were feminists and suffragettes, reflecting the links with the movement. Matfield WI, Kent, established in 1921, had Teresa Sassoon, mother of the wartime poet Siegfried, as a founding member. Although the first presidents of WIs tended to be the ladies of the big houses, their vote ranked equally with that of any other member, and woe betide any woman who thought her social status held any sway. Actually joining filled some potential members with fear, for they had to be nominated and seconded before the application was even considered by the committee. Nellie Clark, who was twenty-five when she joined Hinxworth WI, Hertfordshire in 1938, recalled trembling in case she was not accepted. It is doubtful, though, that Her Majesty Queen Mary felt such trepidation in 1919 when she became the President of Madge Watt's newly formed WI in Sandringham, Norfolk.

Many of the early WIs lacked their own premises, so meetings had to be held in a variety of places, ranging from schools and village halls to private houses and gardens. Schoolrooms were often unpleasant and hot after the children had spent the whole day there, and the old Sunday School could prove very hazardous, judging by the experience of Hinxworth WI,

Opposite: Somerset Federation's superbly decorated version of William Blake's 'Jerusalem', the Women's Institute anthem.

A leaflet promoting the formation of village WIs, with details of how they could help the war effort, c. 1917.

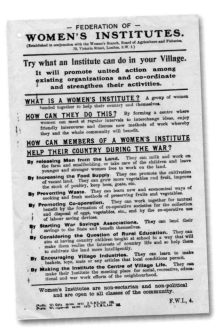

Members of Clothall WI, c. 1930s. The wooden shield reads 'Hertfordshire Federation of Women's Institutes'.

for on more than one occasion a bird's nest up the chimney meant they were smoked out. The 120 members of Girton WI, Cambridge, were lucky to be given a small piece of ground on the High Street in 1920, for which they purchased a prefabricated hut at a Ministry of Munitions sale. Having transported this by horse and cart, along with benches, tables and chairs, to their new home, they then acquired their first 'furnishings', a piano and a clock. An Army Surplus hut bought for £10 in 1923 became home to Ningwood and Shalfleet WI, Isle of Wight, having been erected on land for which they paid a peppercorn rent. Even the local pub was used for meetings, and for many years Badsey WI,

Worcestershire, met first at the Wheatsheaf Inn and later at the Bell Inn. Actually getting to the meetings was often a challenge, and many women, like those who belonged to the Llanfair Waterdine WI, Shropshire, had to walk miles over rough terrain to attend. No wonder that demonstrations of boot mending and classes in re-soling shoes using old rubber tyres were so popular.

Meetings, which lasted about 2½ hours, were held once a month, each member paying 2s a year subscription, a sum that was raised by 6d in 1943. Nellie Clark recalled, in 1997, that it really was a struggle to set this amount aside as the menfolk earned only 30s a week, and did not always see any value in the organisation. To overcome this reluctance, Mrs Rowcroft, a founder member of a Lancashire WI, and some other young women, bribed their husbands with a little extra tobacco. Refreshments were always served, and when the Chipperfield WI, Hertfordshire, was set up in December 1933, Mrs Meehan agreed to be responsible for this duty, charging 1d for a cup of tea, and another 1d for a bun. The rate had

Creech Women's Institute Hall, which was finally closed in March 1993.

A WI member addresses a meeting of the institute in Ashwell Village Hall, 1920s.

The first programme for Ashwell WI, 1918.

increased by 1958, for the ladies attending the newly established WI in Glenavy, Northen Ireland, not only paid 3d for their tea, but they were expected to bring their own cups. Before the advent of the modern kitchen in village halls, cleaning up could be an unpleasant experience, as the Badsey WI members knew only too well, for they had to manage with a chipped enamel bowl on an old wooden table, using cold water heated up on an iron gas stove, and soda as a washing agent.

The programme at every WI meeting followed a set pattern and included a practical, an educational and a social element. According to

Right: Winteringham WI's 'Polly' tea trolley, made from an old pram base with an added super-structure to accommodate the tea accoutrements, 1957.

Rosemary Stephens, a popular demonstration at Merstham WI, Surrey in the 1920s, was one that showed 'ironing a blouse, starching and polishing a gentleman's collar, and last, but most wonderful, crimping with a flat iron.' On another occasion these same ladies were treated to a demonstration by the gas company, who installed stoves free so that they could see 'fried fish, a joint, baked potatoes, apple dumplings, scones and cakes cooked to a turn within the space of an hour.' This was a far cry from the demonstration that took place in 1979, when the ladies were shown how to cook using a microwave.

The best-laid plans sometimes went awry, especially when hop tying and other farming operations took priority, as they did in Lamberhurst, Kent in May 1920. Only two members of the local WI found time to make exhibits for the hat-making competition, making the job of judging by Miss Letch and Miss Earl, two milliners from Sibthorpes in Tunbridge Wells, rather easy. And when Miss Dunk was prevented from demonstrating raffia work to the same WI ladies in March 1925, Miss Harvey and Mrs Champneys stepped into the breach and gave a rather different talk 'on angora and chinchilla rabbit keeping' and talked of forming a rabbit club which besides being 'very interesting, should be remunerative to members.'

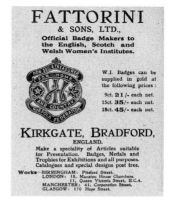

Advertisement for Fattorini & Sons Ltd, official WI badge makers. *Home and Country*, November 1921.

Programme for Bainbridge WI, 1935.

FEBRUARY 19.
" It is never too late to learn."
" Care of the Hair " by Madam Knight, Bradford.
Social Half-hour.
HOSTESSES: Mrs. T. H. Fawcett, Mrs. J. Hopper, Mrs. Hall, Miss Holden, Miss Hodgson.

MARCH 19.
" We learn something by our failures."
Talk by V.C.O. Talk by Mr. Grubb on "Gardening."
W.I. Bulbs.   Judge: Mr. Grubb, Bainbridge.
HOSTESSES: Mrs. R. Hopper, Mrs. Hindle, Mrs. W. Hird, Mrs. Jas. Hodgson, Mrs. John Hodgson, Mrs. J. Iveson.

Wednesday, April 10.
" Second trials often succeed."
" COOKERY." Film in Three Parts by Borwick's Baking Powder Company, Ltd.
Egg collection for Hospital.
HOSTESSES: Mrs. H. Kirkbride, Mrs. M. Kilburn, Mrs. J. T. Leyland, Miss N. Lambert, Mrs. A. Lambert.

MAY 14.
" Nothing is troublesome that we do willingly."
LECTURE on " Drama " by Mr. ABBOTT, Kendal.
Social Half-hour.
HOSTESSES: Mrs. C. Morton, Mrs. Middleton, Miss R. Mason, Mrs. D. Middleton, Mrs. A. Metcalfe.

JUNE 18.
" Success comes in cans, not can'ts."
Cookery : " SALADS " by Miss ANDERSON, Domestic Science Mistress Y.G. School.
Roll Call: Household Hints.
HOSTESSES: Mrs. R. Metcalfe, Mrs. T. Metcalfe, Mrs. J. Metcalfe, Mrs. Orme, Miss Owens, Mrs. Meadows.

For Home and Country.

Bainbridge Women's Institute
Programme, 1935.

MOTTO : " He who shows courtesy reaps friendship, and he who plants kindness gathers love."

Meetings to be held in the Institute on the Third Tuesday in each month, at 7.15 p.m.

PRESIDENT : Mrs. R. C. Shorter.
VICE-PRESIDENTS: Mrs. R. Hopper, Miss Owens.
HON. TREAS.: Mrs. Whyatt.
ASSIST. TREAS.: Mrs. A. Lambert.
HON. SEC.:   JOINT HON. SEC.:
Mrs. Rd. Mason.   Mrs. S. Peacock.
PRESS CORRESPONDENT: Mrs. R. Hopper.

COMMITTEE:
Mrs. T. H. Fawcett, Mrs. W. Hird, Mrs. H. Kirkbride, Mrs. J. T. Leyland, Mrs. T. Metcalfe, Mrs. J. Peacock, Miss R. Routh.

ENT. SUB-COMMITTEE:
Mrs. H. Kirkbride, Mrs. J. T. Leyland Miss Owens, Mrs. Whyatt.

Annual Subscription 2s., payable in February.
Visitors, 6d. each.

JULY.   NO MEETING.

AUGUST 20.
" He who has good health is rich and does not know it."
LECTURE on " HOME NURSING " by Nurse LENG, Askrigg.
Roll Call : Sing, Say, or Pay.
HOSTESSES: Mrs. J. Newton, Mrs. J. Preston, Mrs. J. Peacock, Mrs. F. Paley, Mrs. T. Parrington, Mrs. G. Routh.

T. HISCOCK, PRINTER, HAWES.

Saturday, September 14.
" Wilful waste makes woeful want."
Cookery Demonstration : " How to cook cheap joints of meat " by Miss Burd.
Competition:
Something useful, not to cost more than 6d.
HOSTESSES: Miss E. Routh, Miss M. Raw, Mrs. J. Stevens, Miss A. Raw, Mrs. G. Terry.

OCTOBER 16.
" All for now, nothing for reward."
LANTERN LECTURE given by Mrs. PLACE, Northallerton.
Non-members invited.

OCTOBER 29.
" May we be happy when alone, and cheerful when in company."
Demonstration : " Rug-making " by Messrs. Paton and Baldwins, Halifax.
Social Half-hour.
HOSTESSES: Mrs. H. Weatherald, Miss A. Allen, Mrs. Whyatt, Miss Wrigley, Mrs. G. Atkinson.

NOVEMBER 19.
" When in spite of fun and jest, when Ladies all have done their best, who will buckle to and do the rest— the Gentlemen."
ANNUAL SOCIAL.

DECEMBER 17.
" Better to wear out than rust out."
MEMBERS' EVENING.
Nominations will be taken for the 1936 Committee.
HOSTESSES: Mrs. R. Blades, Mrs. Brown, Miss Chapman, Mrs. Clark, Mrs. T. H. Cockburn, Miss Dinsdale.

JANUARY 21, 1936.
" All's well that ends well."
ANNUAL MEETING. Social Half-hour.
HOSTESSES: The Committee.

An early WI anti-litter campaign, in Inkberrow, Worcesterhire. c. 1933.

Educational activities usually took the form of a lecture, and topics covered a broad canvas. Bee-keeping was especially popular, appearing on the lists at Ampney Crucis, Gloucestershire in 1918, Old Basing, Hampshire in 1920 and Germoe, Truro in 1922. Travel talks were also very well received, for as Catherine Blair recalled:

[There is] nothing the [Scottish] Women's Rural Institute like better.... No wonder. It is fine to be transported to the Alps or the Rockies, to Mexico or the Riviera, to sunny and snowy lands.

Abbots Bromley WI, Staffordshire, were very pleased with the money raised at their Fair in 1927.

Even though the WI was non-party-political, current affairs were not excluded from the educational agenda, and as early as September 1918, the ladies of Ashwell WI, Hertfordshire, listened to a lecture about the use of the vote. This was particularly apposite as just one year later the suffrage movement achieved partial success when the vote was extended to women over thirty.

Some of the ladies of Alstonefield WI in fancy dress, 1920s–30s, outside the old Institute.

From the very early days WIs were not afraid to voice their concerns over the broader issues in education, health and social welfare. The Cambridge Federation was one that earned a reputation for supporting the local County Council on a number of issues, including 'establishing Village Colleges in Cambridgeshire, involving themselves in a "clean milk" campaign at a time when milk-borne tuberculosis was rife, and in rural maternity and bus services.' Then, at the Annual Council Meeting of the Bedfordshire Federation in 1922, a resolution was passed deploring the fact that women police had been disbanded, despite the valuable contribution they had made on the Home Front during the First World War. Nor were environmental matters neglected, as the *Aston Parish News* recalled, for WIs were being urged, in 1927, to pressurise their local County Councils to enforce anti-litter bye-laws, and thus halt 'the growing disfigurement of the countryside.' Nearly three decades later, in 1954, the NF passed a resolution to 'Keep Britain Tidy', laying the foundation for the campaigning group that tackled the increasing litter problem.

Any WIs with concerns about how they filled the social half hour at the end of meetings needed only to look at the NF helpful handbook, which consisted of 'fifty pages of practical suggestions for use in the social life of the Women's Institute suitable for all eventualities.' Some activities could prove quite a challenge, as a cheery spinster who belonged to an SWRI discovered. When each member was asked, in advance, to bring a man to the Fancy Dress Dance, she responded: 'Here I have been trying to get a man for twenty years – and the Rural expects me to get one in a fortnight.'

FROM FARM AND GARDEN TO KITCHEN AND STALL

We have to prevent hunger – every ounce of food which can be grown in this country must be grown, and every woman who can give a hand in this vastly important work must give a hand.

Miss Meriel Talbot, Director of the Women's Branch of the Food Production Department of the Board of Agriculture.

By the time these words were spoken at an NF meeting in October 1917, the WIs had already applied themselves to making the most of local produce, allowing nothing to go to waste. Conserving fruit was a novel concept in England in 1916, but thanks to Mr Yerburgh, the President of the AOS, six fruit-sterilising outfits were imported from the USA, precipitating a bigger demand for this 'modern' equipment, and for demonstrations to be given to nearly all the existing 199 branches. Jam making, which was to earn the WIs a formidable reputation, was also simmering away, exemplified by a WI factory operating in Cirencester around 1916, and another in Wye. Writing in *Home and Country* in July 1919, Mrs Dunstan attributed the main success of this latter venture to the 'copper':

We could make nearly one hundred pounds of jam in it at a time, and as the fire would burn anything such as rubbish, peels etc. our fuel bill for making six and a half tons of jam was less than two pounds.

'Waste not, want not' was a frequently invoked motto, so that when there was a glut of plums in Cambridgeshire in October 1930, *Home and Country* was able to inform readers that Eversden WI had produced over one and a half gross of cans (more than 216) using the Williamson's Hand Sealing Machine.

The question of how to deal with the excess produce from members' gardens and allotments was solved in Criccieth, Caernarvonshire in early summer 1916, when, as Constance Davies recalled, the fledgling WI started a small country market stall. But the real impetus for WI markets started in Lewes, East Sussex on 14 December 1919, when a number of local WIs opened their own co-operative venture. Generally accepted as the first WI market, Sussex initially sold only what members had grown, but the facility was soon extended to include smallholders, cottagers and ex-servicemen, enabling them to dispose of their excess produce profitably. At its height the market was selling goods from twenty-three local WIs, and anyone could become a shareholder. The NF watched the growth of markets in other CFs, including East Kent, Berkshire and Buckinghamshire, and in 1932 decided the time had come to encourage expansion nationally. The Carnegie United Kingdom Trust (CUKT) provided a grant, a marketing organiser was appointed and a handbook produced, and by the end of the year nine CFs had County Marketing Societies. These early markets became the springboard for WI Country Markets Ltd and in 1993, with more than 500 markets in England and Wales and an annual turnover of £10.4 million, the organisation became independent of the NF.

Ideally suited to WIs, canning machines like the Easiwork Home Canner, on sale in 1933, made fruit preservation a much quicker and more profitable process.

Recipe books were produced from the early days, growing by the twenty-first century into a hugely successful stand-alone business venture. Members, like those of the SWRI, the first edition of whose book appeared in 1925, contributed their favourite recipe, some of which were unnerving. As the *Aston Parish News* wrote in 1997: 'Dinner for Five Persons for Three Days from Sheep's Pluck' was as unappetising a thought as the recipe for 'Brain Cakes', made from sheep brains boiled in milk, sent in by a lady from Largo WI.

Anyone buying produce at this market stall run by Holmer WI, Herefordshire in 1943, was reminded of food shortages by posters that warned 'Someone forgot that food costs lives' and 'If you didn't want it, why did you take it?'

BEDFORD COUNTY FEDERATION OF WOMEN'S INSTITUTES.

Exhibition & Sale

OF

HOMECRAFTS

AT

ST. PETER'S HALLS, BEDFORD,

ON

WEDNESDAY, SEPT. 28th, 1927,

From 11.30 to 7 o'clock.

TO BE OPENED AT 2.30 BY

Mrs. JOHN BUCHAN,

Who will present the Cups and Certificates.

ADMISSION: For Members of Women's Institutes wearing Badge or producing Membership Card, 3d.

For the general public, 1/-

TEAS 9d. under the management of MRS. H. A. HARDING.

Hon. Exhibition Secretary: MISS CAMPION, 59, Foster Hill Road, Bedford.
Hon. Exhibition Treasurers:
MR. & MRS. WALTER SHEPHERD, Union Bank Chambers, Bedford.

Poster for a homecrafts exhibition in Bedfordshire.

Handicraft advertisement, *Home and Country*, November 1921. With leather work, and especially glove-making, such a popular handicraft, manufacturers were keen to advertise in *Home and Country*, and to offer the WIs skins at special rates.

LEATHER WORK FOR INSTITUTES.

Gloving Leathers
in Chamois, White Washable and Colours.

Art Leathers
in Sheep and Calf for decorative work

Suede and Grain Finished Leathers
in every shade for Hats, Bags, Moccasins, and Fancy Work of all kinds.

WASH LEATHERS FOR HOUSE & GARAGE USE.

Special Terms to Women's Institutes.
Sample Skins sent on approval.

Purchase direct from

G. W. RUSSELL & SON, Ltd.,
Leather Manufacturers,
HITCHIN.

HANDICRAFTS AND THE WI

From the moment that the fifty-three existing WIs took the plunge and exhibited a small handicraft display at a National Economy Exhibition in Hyde Park, London, in the summer of 1917, craftwork and the WI became inseparable bedfellows, not least because it provided an opportunity to save rural crafts. Early toy-making caught the imagination of the Essex Institutes and in 1918 the WI Toy Society was established, primarily to produce a stuffed rabbit called Cuthbert. This commercial venture provided scope for employment for WI members and wounded soldiers, but competition from abroad, combined with a fall in the standard of goods produced, soon heralded the demise of the society. Toys were still made, as were baskets, gloves and more, with certain institutes becoming experts in a particular craft. Inez Jenkins records how Miss Phyllis Hardman of Northaw WI in Hertfordshire was the first WI member ever to make a pair of fur gloves, using home-cured rabbit skin, exhibited in a 'something out of nothing' category at the first exhibition. Northaw led the way in the WI practice of furcraft, and in 1919 their president, Lady Pollock, took the plunge and formed a Furcraft Guild. There were sound words of advice from the Ampney Crucis instructor, who taught members of nine other WIs how to skin rabbits and to dry and stretch the pelts, for they were cautioned that they should 'remove the entrails (paunch) before skinning, to prevent "something nasty" happening.'

The WIs in Oxfordshire were also very active on the handicrafts scene and in 1921, as Pat Kirkham describes, they organised a travelling exhibition of their handiwork. Ticehurst WI in Sussex gained a reputation for the smocked dresses and children's knitwear they produced, even advertising them for sale in *The Lady*. A seemingly endless variety of crafts was taught and

Bedfordshire
Federation ladies
weaving baskets,
1940s.

Lerwick SWRI
rug-making group,
carding and
spinning,
c. 1926–27.

demonstrated to WI members up and down the land, ranging from cobbling to crochet, from basket-making to blacksmithing, tailoring, straw-hat making, upholstery, weaving, patchwork, rug making and more. The 'very practical lecture on coats into frocks' which the Annscroft and District WI had in February 1938 stood them in good stead once clothes rationing came in during the Second World War.

Having reached a decision not to pursue crafts on a commercial basis, the NF decided, in 1920, to establish their Guild of Learners to 'assist in bringing the best instruction in handicrafts within the reach of villages.' When the first National Handicraft Exhibition was held at the Victoria and Albert Museum in 1922, the quality of the exhibits reflected the prestige of the venue, for only entries of the very highest standard were accepted. And there was a big difference between this and the previous craft exhibitions held in 1918 and 1920, for, as Inez Jenkins records, this time there were no goods for sale, no prizes and no competitions. With the paradigm now set, the next exhibition, held in 1924 at the Drapers' Hall in the City of London, proved to be an even greater success, for the shortcomings in design and colour, commented upon in 1922, were a thing of the past, and the results were outstanding.

WI embroidery being admired at the Ridgmont Exhibition, c. 1940s.

The lack of space in the Indian Pavilion of the Imperial Institute, the venue for the 1927 exhibition, meant that the number of exhibits was restricted, but this served to raise the standard of entries to an even higher level. According to Inez Jenkins, this was the first year that gold stars were awarded, with fifty-four items achieving the accolade. With war looming, the last triennial handicraft exhibition held in peacetime took place in October 1938, and much to the delight of the secretary, it made a very healthy profit of £100, rather than the £80 on a budget of £3,000 which, according to Cecily McCall, had been anticipated.

This beautiful hand-embroidered banner depicts the Maid of Kent and the local produce of apples, pears, barley and dog roses. This WI closed in 1939.

WI colour printing class, Hereford, 1946.

ARTS AND LEISURE

'Jerusalem' is a happy choice, for the delegates sing hopefully of the New Jerusalem which every Institute member is helping to build.

General Secretary, recorded in *Home And Country* (n.d.)

MUSIC

It is hardly surprising, as the very first WI was formed in Wales, that music and singing would become an integral part of the organisation. At the inaugural meeting at Llanfair in 1915, Inez Jenkins describes how members were treated to 'selections on the harp played by Miss Thomas' while the ladies of the WI in Trefnant were entertained with 'music selections'. But the WI ladies from Chilworth, Surrey, wanted to do the singing rather than be sung to, as Sylvia Drew made clear in her letter to *Home and Country* in September 1919. She asked how best to 'draw out the musical talent of our Institute' and suggested that a 'scheme of simple competitions of folk and part songs might be welcomed.' Choirs began to be formed, with the Shropshire Federation earning the distinction of being the founders of the first WI music sub-committee in 1922. By good fortune they invited Mr Leslie, an amateur musician of Llansantffraid, Powys, to advise them. One thing led to another, and before long he was conducting singing schools at CFs around the country, contributing articles on choirs and music to *Home and Country* as well as helping the NF bring out the original *Women's Institute Song Book*. Mr Leslie also had a hand in the adoption of Blake's 'Jerusalem' as the WI anthem. Grace Hadow wanted a suitable unifying song for the annual meetings, and was a great admirer of this piece, perhaps because it had been the Suffragettes' hymn. At Mr Leslie's suggestion, a special arrangement of Sir Hubert Parry's setting was written by Sir Walford Davies, and sung at the AGM in 1924.

The first WI choral competition was held in East Sussex in 1923 but the WIs were soon complaining that their musical progress was being held back by the difficulty they had in finding competent conductors. This problem was resolved two years later when the CUKT and the NF started a joint scheme

Opposite:
The ladies
of St Giles,
Shrewsbury,
enjoying a game
of musical chairs,
1 January 1954.

27

Hawes WI concert programme for March 1932.

Welsh WI ladies practising a script or singing at the Merioneth Women's Institute drama school, 1 April 1954.

Hawes Women's Institute.

Concert,

In the Market Hall, Hawes,

Friday, March 4, 1932,

To commence at 7.30 p.m.

Reserved Seats, 1s.6d.

for training conductors and producers of drama. Following the success of the first NF School for Conductors held in November 1931, one participant was prompted to write to *Home and Country* in January 1932:

From Mr Read we begin (*sic*) to learn the mysteries of controlling a conducting stick and by the afternoon, by dint of practice against our neighbour's arm and ribs, were engaging ourselves conducting in fine style.

DRAMA

WI ladies all over the country were also firmly engaged in pageants, carnivals and theatrical productions, and hidden talent was being unleashed at a rate of knots. Innumerable plays were performed,

sometimes at the end of the monthly meeting, such as Codicote in Hertfordshire's 'splendid' rendition of *The Gipsies' Holiday* in October 1923. Ampney Crucis WI boasted a team of black and white minstrels, and the overriding memory of this was the difficulty members had removing their make-up afterwards. The year after the first national Drama Festival in 1928, Bedford Park was the venue for a spectacular production of *The Masque of the Lady Margaret*. All the costumes were designed and made by the Bedfordshire WI members, and there was a cast of hundreds from across the county.

A very early WI carnival float in Wales.

Barmouth WI carnival float, c. 1930s.

WEDNESDAY, 30th January 1935

Dunbar W.R.I. Amateur Dramatic Society

PRESENTS

"THE BRIDE"

COMEDY

(GERTRUDE JENNINGS)

Characters—

Susan (lady's maid)	. .	Jean Wight
Mrs Irving (bride's mother)	. . .	Mrs Hardy
Judith (bridesmaid)	. . .	Mrs Leggat
Joyce (bride)	. . . .	Maud Brown
Madam Grace (French dressmaker)	.	Jean Myles
Miss Sparrow (faded woman of 45)	. .	Mrs Purves

Period—Present   *Scene*—Bedroom

Producer—Mrs Hardy

Stage Manager—Miss Barlas

NOTES

Programme
and cast list
for *The Bride*,
30 January 1935.

OUTINGS

WI members always had a liking for outings, and Mrs Curley Brown, a member of Singleton WI in Somerset, summed up their significance when she said 'I have always wanted to travel, and now it is going to be possible through the WI.' In many instances it was the very first time that some women had ventured out of their village, or, as in rural East Lothian, Scotland, stepped far from their cottages, except for the annual Fair Day. Many early trips were quite close to home, and indeed the distance that members of rural SWRIs travelled was, according to Catherine Blair, governed by how far the motor buses could travel in a day. When thirty ladies from the Lamberhurst WI attended the Maidstone Exhibition in 1920, the committee decided to 'hire a conveyance from Autocar Services Ltd, price £8 10s, and charge members 5s, empty seats to be paid for by Institute funds.' The outing was well worthwhile, for their entries won first prize for butter, second for furcraft and third and fifth for knitting. Some years later, in 1936, when the ladies of Merstham WI went to Windsor, there was a curious charging scheme of 4s per seat, 3s for a child or 8s for three bottoms on two seats. But possibly the most special outing took place in 1937, when a thousand

SWRI production
of *The Bride*,
30 January 1935.

Barford WI ladies on a charabanc outing to the Peak District, c. 1925.

lucky Institute members travelled to London to enjoy a wonderful view of the great Coronation procession of King George VI and Queen Elizabeth from a special stand provided for them by the Government. By now the WI had 5,500 institutes and 318,000 members, and it was these whom Lady Denman addressed in a broadcast on 21 July 1937, marking the twenty-first anniversary of the organisation. Her words were recorded by Inez Jenkins:

> The experience of twenty-one years' work shows that we can do something to add to the happiness of the country-side. I know you will agree with me when I say that there is no job that is better worth doing.

With war on the horizon, Lady Denman's sentiments certainly rang true, for the WI contribution to the war effort was tremendous, and was undertaken with a good spirit and an open heart.

Ladies of Pattingham WI, Shropshire, posing before they leave on their coach outing, c. 1936.

THE SECOND WORLD WAR

WIs have been the means of seeking out hitherto unexpected proofs of the resourcefulness, the capacity, the intelligence and the initiative of our countrywomen. Everywhere they have put themselves at the disposal of the communities they serve.

Cosmo Gordon Lang, Archbishop of Canterbury.

When the Archbishop of Canterbury wrote this in 1940, the WIs were well entrenched in war work. Even though there were some new branches formed, including one in Guarlford, near Malvern, Worcestershire in May 1941, overall membership numbers were reduced and the Lancashire Federation, for example, had lost nearly 450 members by then. But despite this decline, members made a massive contribution to the war effort, which was considered important enough for the official war artists Evelyn Dunbar and Elsie Hewland, the Ministry of Information, and J. B. Priestley in his book, *British Women Go To War*, published in 1943, to record their activities for posterity. Even though sentiments like those expressed by the speaker at the Sudbury WI, Middlesex, annual produce show in July 1940 – that it 'needed no war to wake up the WIs ... they were already doing fine work in keeping men and families fit and living up to their motto "For Home and Country"' – the NF felt the need to issue WIs with a set of guidelines, all of which reflected the need for a community spirit.

There was a variety of reasons for WIs to suspend official meetings during wartime. The blackout was certainly an obstacle to evening arrangements, so some institutes moved their meetings to the afternoon. Others battled with the problem of heating perishingly cold village halls when coal was rationed and scarce. Many, like Ovingham WI, in the Tyne valley, simply lost their village hall in 1939 when it was commandeered for the billeting of soldiers. And even though Kingston Bagpuize with Southmoor WI in Oxfordshire had their village hall turned into a canteen

Opposite:
Sandon WI helping
the Red Cross
at Sandon Hall,
making bandages
and mending
clothing and
bedding. Standing
at back left is
Lady Harrowby,
Fifth Countess.

Members of Etchingham WI celebrate their silver anniversary, 1944. This picture was taken outside Fletcher's House, Rye, East Sussex.

for the Forces based nearby, when a Forces cinema was built on adjacent land the ladies put their catering skills to good use by serving refreshments every night of the week from 6 p.m. to 10 p.m. There were members who objected to wartime meetings on the grounds that they were of no value to the war effort, but it was generally felt that these two hours were a golden opportunity to relax away from the pressures of home and daily responsibilities, and, as such, were a great morale booster. And despite wartime austerity, WIs still managed to celebrate their anniversaries, as Etchingham, East Sussex proved in 1944, even producing a cake for the occasion.

Much more emphasis was put upon practical demonstrations at monthly meetings, with members receiving lessons in first aid and air raid precaution or, like the members of Badsey WI, meeting 'Resuscitating Annie' for the first time. Along with many others, the ladies of Longstone WI, Derbyshire, were given instructions in hay-box cooking, the economical use of food, the re-footing of lisle stockings and dress renovation. Besides this, members were often shown Ministry of Information films at meetings including *The Danger of Invasion* and *The Necessity of Saving for the War Effort*.

EVACUEES

Despite all the preparations, the reality of helping with the evacuation of children from the cities took many WIs by surprise and most rural members were shocked by the poor standards of health, hygiene, diet and education of many of the evacuees, children and mothers alike. This prompted the NF to try and do something to effect a long-term improvement in the conditions for urban children and before long, 1,700 institutes were taking part in a survey, published in 1940 as *Town Children Through Country Eyes*. Writing about their impressions of evacuation, one member recorded the chief difficulties with children from Islington, London, being the '... great prevalence of bed-wetting and other insanitary habits.' Another wrote of a five-year-old girl from Liverpool who said that 'one day she would like to have beer and cheese for supper.' Yet another child, a boy from Salford, Lancashire, was described as 'very thin, had never had a bath before, his ribs looked as if black-leaded, suffered from head lice.' That the health, weight and manners of most children improved from being in the country was a great tribute to the foster families, which included WI members, and as the report added, many of them became so attached to the youngsters that they dreaded their departure.

Children evacuated from Bristol, arriving in Kingsbridge, Devon, 1940.

FOOD

Food production was next on the priority list and WI members took to this like ducks to water. They were out acquiring allotments and organising meetings to advise on the importance of home-grown vegetables and community gardening even before the Government's 'Dig for Victory' campaign swung into action. Nationally, the Produce Guild, for which, according to M. Morgan, there was a 1s annual subscription, was also established in 1939 to encourage food production and self-sufficiency, and the Yorkshire branch was very honoured when HRH The Princess Royal joined its guild in early 1940. Nearby, the Lancashire Federation Produce Guild boasted 624 members from thirty-four local institutes, and in 1941, responded to the call to grow more onions by joining the NF Onion Scheme. Any surplus onions were distributed to areas where there was a shortage, and this prompted Miss Hibbert-Ware to propose that her local WI in Girton form an 'Onion Club'. Rearing animals played an equally important part in being self-sufficient, and a

Ladies of Springfield WI, Essex, with home-grown produce for sale, August 1941.

series of articles appeared in *Home and Country* with the delightful title of 'Betty in the Hen House' which spelled out the dos and don'ts of keeping chickens. Members were also strongly encouraged to keep rabbits for meat and fur, goats for butter, milk and cheese, and bees for honey, as well as running pig clubs. According to Sybil Everitt, 1,000 members of the Produce Guild in Gloucestershire participated in the NF Seed Collection Scheme, distributing plants and seeds which were sent from the USA to various societies and clubs in the county. When Aylsham WI in Norfolk received a gift of tomato seeds from Canada in 1943, Mrs Ewing volunteered to raise them, and when they were ready some weeks later, sixty-four members each received two plants. Others, including twenty members from Merstham WI, volunteered to give part-time help on farms and smallholdings.

To supplement the labour shortage, the Essex Federation was asked to form an Emergency Land Corps, and its members worked on the land along with some conscientious objectors and a few soldiers who were waiting to

Bedfordshire Federation ladies with fruit they have gathered, c. 1944.

go off to fight in the war. Collecting fruit and vegetables was a commonplace activity for WI members, but there were also many institutes who gathered rosehips for syrup production, with the 131 pounds collected by the ladies of Deddington and North Aston WI, Oxfordshire, far exceeding the 28 pounds which Fovant and Sutton Mandeville WI, Wiltshire, managed to harvest in 1941. But Leicestershire and Rutland Federation topped the lot, and at the end of the war received a certificate for having collected the greatest weight.

AND IS THERE JAM FOR TEA?

Jam making, for which WI members seemed to have a natural gift, became an institution under the Ministry of Food Fruit Preservation Scheme, with fruit preservation centres established all over the country. The enterprise was far more demanding than non-practitioners realised, as Rosemary Stephens detailed in her record of Merstham WI: 'Jars had to be official Ministry of Food one pound jars, filled to the brim. Greaseproof paper tops on, secured with fine twine in a special knot, correct labels used' – to say nothing of standing and constantly stirring boiling cauldrons of jam, then lifting and pouring the contents into the sterilised jars. In 1940 alone, the Bedfordshire Federation produced 44,800 pounds of preserves using about 9 tons of sugar. This was a precious commodity in wartime and had to be obtained at the cheapest possible price, so that smart WIs like Ashwell 'took advantage of the cheap rate for sugar offered by the NF for early ordering of sugar in October 1939, and on a bulk order of five hundredweight made a profit of one pound.'

In the early war years canning produce became possible when machines were sent to Britain from the USA and Canada. Washington WI in West Sussex ran its first fruit-canning day in 1940, but did not become the owner of its own machine until 1947. Gloucestershire Federation was more fortunate and, according to Sybil Everitt, received twenty-two machines from Canada via the NF in 1941, which were distributed to areas where there was a glut of fruit. When more arrived from abroad in 1942, Gloucestershire was allocated a further ten machines, two of which were loaned to local agricultural hostels. Even though 1944 was a bad year for fruit, Gloucestershire maintained excellent figures and was third in the list of producing counties. The WI ladies of Bardney, Lincolnshire, were also in the fortunate position of having their own canning apparatus, and, demonstrating a true community spirit, they took it around the village so that everyone could can their surplus fruit.

Storing jam presented some WIs, like Langton Maltravers in Dorset, with a moral dilemma. Even though they had organised three storage depots, the members were concerned about its safety:

In those strange days, when parachutes were expected by day and night, a serious problem arose. Was it wiser to hide one's store of jam under the floor or somehow sealed up in a quarry hole or was it better to imitate a Jael (a biblical character) housewife who kept a hammer ready for a last minute smashing, in the hopes of the dire effects of powdered glass on jam-starved Germans?

Many WIs, like Ashton-under-Edge in the Vale of Evesham, did not start up canning clubs until after the war, but by 1948 this particular WI could proudly claim that during their twice-weekly sessions, twenty-five members had processed 2,500 cans. Each can was coded to denote the owner and contents.

KEEPING UP MORALE

The WIs went a long way to keep up the morale of their villages during wartime, often by engaging the community in all manner of activities. Entertaining evacuees and members of the Forces was a popular way of

Two Bedfordshire WI ladies pouring and straining fruit for jam making, c.1944.

encouraging neighbours and friends to join in and when Ningwoood and Shalfleet WI on the Isle of Wight put on an evening on 6 January 1941, they had over a hundred people enjoying team games, dancing and an amusing recitation, as well as refreshments.

Knitting comforts for the Forces was especially popular with WI ladies, and to help in this endeavour, members were encouraged to register with the NF to obtain 24 ounces of wool for knitting, coupon-free. Ningwood and Shalfleet WI, for one, produced an incredible 974 garments. The *Daily Mail* went one better with a scheme, to which many WI members subscribed, whereby special wool was provided free of charge to be knitted into sea-boot stockings. Everybody was drawn into the 'knitting circle', from school children in Carlton-le-Moorland, Lincolnshire who were taught by Miss Harby of the local WI, to the men who were handed a pair of knitting needles.

WIs up and down the country made mattresses stuffed with wood shavings for the army camps, salvaged waste paper and made minesweepers' gloves, to say nothing of the industrious women like those of Guarlford WI who made camouflage nets, managing to produce nine in the three months between December 1943 and February 1944. Many WIs,

Mrs Camp and Mrs Wallace, members of Ashwell WI, judging produce at a WI show in Wrestlingworth, Bedfordshire, c. 1952.

such as Wootton and Sandford in Oxfordshire, were engaged in more mundane but no less valuable activities, which included distributing ration books, orange juice and cod liver oil, collecting eggs for the local hospital, dishing out milk and cocoa to the boys and girls in their villages and setting up a baby clinic. To encourage a greater sense of community, members of Billesdon WI in Leicestershire took it upon themselves to teach ballroom dancing to Italian prisoners of war.

The 'Letter Friend Scheme', set up after the outbreak of war, was extremely successful, and as Inez Jenkins recorded, a thousand postal friendships were established within a year, mainly between WI members in England and Wales, but also with country women in the USA. It was thanks to Miss Wood, their Consultative Council member, that the Lancashire Federation's letter scheme won them the accolade of being second highest in the country in 1941. More unusually, in early 1941, the ladies of the Literary Circle of the Loughton WI in Essex came up with the novel idea of launching a quarterly magazine, *The Venture*, devoted to the activities of the circle. Painstakingly handwritten and colour illustrated, contributions were wide-ranging, from the misuse of sugar meant for fruit preservation, to poems, stories and reports on visits to other WIs, all of which demonstrated the remarkable skill, education and depth of knowledge among the women contributors.

FUNDRAISING

Besides all of this, there was fundraising to do, with money from flag days, whist drives, concerts and socials going to, among others, Red Cross funds, ambulance funds, air raid distress funds and National Savings campaigns. The latter were to encourage civilians to save their money in Government accounts, such as War, Savings or Defence Bonds and Savings Certificates and when Guarlford WI, Wiltshire, held a garden party in June 1942, the prizes took the form of savings stamps.

During 1941, Ashwell WI held a 'War Weapons Week' and were responsible for the Messerschmitt that was on view. By getting members to pay a small sum to sit at 'the receipt of vision' they managed to raise £21. In 1943 it was decided the national scheme would be a 'Wings for Victory' week, themed around raising funds to purchase more bombers for the nation to take the fight to the enemy homeland. Many WIs raised money for Mrs Churchill's 'Aid for Russia Fur Scheme'; others made more than 2,000 assorted rabbit-fur-lined coats, waistcoats, hoods and caps, which were sent to the women of Russia through the Red Cross. With clothes rationing introduced on 1 June 1941, 'Make Do and Mend' became a frequently invoked motto, aided by the NF's 6d booklet, *Thrift Crafts*, published in 1942, with its wealth of information and directions for recycling goods, including

making excellent beds for shelters and ARP points from motor tyre tube. It would have needed a very hard-hearted WI member to ignore the sentiments in Miss Somerville's foreword in which she implored:

> Should any fortunate housewife find that she possesses enough rugs, blankets, quilts and clothing for her own use, let her remember those whose homes have been entirely swept away and that must be rebuilt without and within from the very foundations.

As the war neared an end, WIs were called upon to help people in liberated Europe. Small woollen garments were needed for babies, and although the members of Aylsham WI had resisted guaranteeing being able to knit the 3½ pounds of wool required each month, they nevertheless made a commendable contribution to this appeal. Mrs Spink was able to report that between 3 August 1944 and 2 August 1945 she and the other members had knitted 72 pairs of socks and 165 garments, which included shawls, coats, pilches (a cover to go over a cloth nappy) and jerseys, all of which had been safely dispatched abroad.

Above: Ladies of Bishopthorpe WI knitting socks for seamen. One member recalled the wool being very oily.

Opposite: Newtown WI with their only male knitter, seen here in 1939 wearing his handmade balaclava.

A NEW ERA DAWNS: THE 1940s TO 1960s

Victory and the return to peacetime were well worth celebrating, and along with fêtes and carnivals that re-emerged from the dark days of war, enthusiastic WIs like Newton-by-the-Sea in Northumberland organised 'welcome home' parties with a tea and a dance. Outings, which had been curtailed mainly due to petrol rationing, were soon resumed, and it was an eager group of thirty-three ladies and their friends from Deddington WI, which embarked upon a long-anticipated visit to Stratford-upon-Avon in August 1945, only to find the shops and tearooms closed as a result of the celebrations for Victory in Japan Day. Food rationing was still a part of everyday life, and during 1948 the NF ran 'Operation Produce', the aim being for every WI member, countrywide, to produce an extra 10 pounds in weight of food. The Buckinghamshire members were so successful that Lord Woolton, the wartime Minister of Food, performed the opening ceremony at their Produce Exhibition in Aylesbury.

Members continued to devote free time to helping in the local community, and international relations, already fostered with the Letter Friend Scheme, grew after the end of the war. Many WIs, including Annscroft and District WI in Shropshire, were the fortunate recipients of parcels from abroad, and while they used some of the goods sent to them by the Country Women's Association of Australia to make their twentieth birthday cake, Guarlford WI held a ballot among members for their gift.

There was a renewed energy in establishing groups, and, thanks to another grant from the CUKT, the Channel Islands were able to start their own groups, the first of which was St Aubin and St Clements, formed in 1947. The Isle of Man soon followed suit in 1949, the same year that the Jersey Federation was established. But being a member became more expensive, as Mrs Hussey, of Mithian WI, Cornwall, had to announce to her members in 1949. The subscription was rising from 2s 6d to 3s 6d per year, of which Mithian retained 1s, the County 1s 6d and the National Federation 1s. In 1950 someone in this WI was beginning to get tough and proposed that 'those who have not paid [their subscription] by January 31st will be fined the amount of 3d.'

Opposite:
Tree planting by Church Village WI in Pontypridd, Wales, to celebrate the Festival of Britain, 16 November 1951.

45

Badsey WI visit
to London, 1950s.

A member of
Chirk WI receiving
a prize for her
spring onions,
1 September 1954.

Colton WI
Produce Guild,
20 August 1960.

Salop Federation
Autumn
Conference,
1 November 1950.

Meanwhile, a very important event took place on 24 September 1948, with the opening of Denman College, a Georgian house set in acres of land in what is now Oxfordshire, as the WI's very own college. Named in honour of the first chairman, Lady Denman, who had just retired after thirty years, the college began by offering two levels of short residential courses in subjects which reflected all the special interests of members.

Drama, music and singing were still at the heart of the WI, and every decade was marked by a series of national events and new challenges. When the first national WI Music Festival was held in 1950, a choir of nearly 3,000 women sang a specially commissioned cantata, *Folk Songs of the Four Seasons*, by Ralph Vaughan Williams. One member of Pickering WI was almost reduced to tears, as Lorna Gibson recorded:

Queen Elizabeth at the Hertfordshire Federation Rally at Knebworth House, 1949.

Hilton WI ladies dressed up as Madame Garnetti's puppets for *The Children's Opera*, written and arranged by Angelica and Amaryllis Garnett in 1951.

Words fail to do justice to the experience shared by all who were privileged to share the inspiration and uplift of the great occasion .... Standing in silence to sing Jerusalem the effect was overwhelming and vivid.

On the drama front, new groups sprang up, including the one started by Mrs Daphne Bell of Badsey WI in 1951. Lacking a proper stage, the first

Cottingham and Middleton WI Choir, 1961–2, having just won a trophy at the Oundle Music Festival for the second year running.

Bedfordshire
Federation
Danish Dancing
competition,
October 1955.

performances took place on an improvised construction of trestle-table tops perched on wooden beer crates. Authenticity was crucial, so much so that when, in one play, a part called for a chicken to be plucked, a real chicken was actually plucked on stage.

The Festival of Britain in 1951 was aimed at raising the nation's spirits and the WIs grasped the opportunity of celebrating by putting on a vast range of activities. Locally, the members of Smarden WI, Kent, decided to extend a week's hospitality to a party of twenty-five visiting Norwegian women, whom the minutes described as 'charming … as they paraded [down the village street] to church, wearing their picturesque national costume.' In Preston, Lancashire, the local federation held a Folk Song and Dance Festival, with massed choirs of 465 singers and dancers from thirty WIs, while the West Sussex Women's Institute held a Festival of Good Entertainment. Nationally, the organisers of the 1951 Ideal Homes Exhibition gave every member the unique opportunity of helping to design, equip and furnish the ideal WI house, suitable for a rural family of mother, father and three children. Contributions had been invited the previous year, and the full plans were shown in the March 1951 issue of *Home and Country*, with photos of the house and completed interior included the following month. The house was a highlight of the exhibition and some 37,000 WI ladies were among the 140,000 people who passed through it.

Members of
Amlwch Women's
Institute at their
Christmas party
celebrations in
1953, dressed up
as various queens
across the
centuries.

Lady Brunner, the NF Chair, was the prime mover behind the idea for a WI house to be exhibited at the 1951 Ideal Home Exhibition. The house was designed by the architect Lionel Brett (later Lord Esher), and incorporated suggestions from some six thousand WI members who had responded to a questionnaire sent out by the NF. The first scale model was stolen, and when Maxwell Wright, a professional model maker, was commissioned to make a replacement, he was asked to create it in two separate pieces, so that each floor could be seen in detail, complete with furnishings.

Ladies from Winster WI at their burger bar, early 1960s.

Market Lavington WI celebrates its twenty-first birthday, 1960.

When it came to coronation year in 1953, WIs held a ballot for tickets to attend, and put on a wide variety of events across the country ranging from parties and pageants to the purchase of commemorative village seats. In Milton Malsor, Northamptonshire, the £33 profit from a garden party was used to buy a coronation seat for Malzor Lane.

During the 1960s, while local WIs celebrated birthdays, ran stalls at local fairs and enjoyed art classes *en plein air*, the first National Art Exhibition, 'Painting for Pleasure', was held at the recently opened galleries of the Federation of British Artists in Pall Mall, London in 1963. Then there was the staging of the specially commissioned opera, *The Brilliant and the Dark*, based on the lives of British women during the past 1,000 years, at the second national WI Music Festival at the Royal Albert Hall in London on 3 June 1969. Preliminary county and regional auditions for soloists, choirs and pianists were held well in advance, but as Sybil Everitt recalls, the 1,000 women singers who were

eventually chosen only met for the first time at 2.30 p.m. to rehearse for the first evening performance at 5 p.m.

The greatest cause for celebration was the NF Golden Jubilee year in 1965, commemorated by innumerable events. One of these was the 'Golden Market' mounted at the Ideal Home Exhibition at Olympia in March, an occasion which a member of Welham Green WI, Hertfordshire, remembered only too well. She told a *Sunday Telegraph* reporter of the panic on the first morning, when the ladies of Welham Green WI were greeted by 'thick snow

Bedfordshire WI ladies watch their instructor sketching a tree, 2 July 1963.

Bedfordshire Federation Golden Jubilee Choir 1969.

A WI group visiting a textile factory, c. 1950–60.

at 6.30 a.m. – engine [of the Traveller car] would not start ...' But they did make it in time, and were very proud when, at last, having queued behind other vans, and gone up in the lifts with a huge metal goods trolley, their produce was on sale. There were innumerable local events too, such as the Golden Jubilee rally held by the Buckinghamshire Federation at Cliveden, attended by more than 7,000 members.

The other great experience that year was the special Garden Party held at Buckingham Palace on 31 May. The Queen invited one member from every institute to attend, and ballots were held up and down the country. Mrs Wallace, whose name was pulled out of Hertfordshire Federation's hat, recalled the excitement of travelling by coach to London, and of catching a glimpse of the Queen as she passed by on her way from taking tea, 'a petite figure in cerise coat and matching hat, just an ordinary WI member like ourselves yet so serene and calm, a veritable Queen.'

At grass-roots level, scrapbooks were painstakingly compiled by WIs up and down the country, recording, for posterity, village and WI life in words and pictures. A fine example was the Hertingfordbury scrapbook, which describe how some of the members 'help in hospital driving, run the outpatients' canteen and hospital Red Cross shop …', while others 'carry out visits to the blind.' Up north, the SWRI was also celebrating its fiftieth anniversary, and Ewes and Clarebrand WIs were among the participants who produced a village history in a competition to commemorate this great occasion. Across the sea, Mrs Heron, the outgoing President of Glenavy WI, declared, as a tribute to the success of the group, that 'the ship has been well and truly launched.'

The downside to the 1960s was the foot and mouth epidemic, which in late 1967 brought regular WI meetings to a standstill. The Shropshire Federation ceased meetings in November and did not hold any meetings again until April 1968. The county suffered again in July 1968 when two days of tropical storms affected the electricity supply, but, as Carole Morgan recorded, 'Mrs Carswell did make us all a cup of tea by means of boiling the kettle on the fire.'

Market Lavington
WI meeting, 1960.

FROM THE 1970s TO THE NEW MILLENNIUM

D ENMAN COLLEGE was thriving both in size – the Queen Mother opened a new teaching centre in 1970 – and in the scope of the courses on offer. Elsie Riddick, a member of Alperton and Wembley WI, Middlesex recalled, in 2003, winning a bursary to attend Denman in the 1970s, describing the experience as:

> … most interesting, but very hard work all the time. But I met WI members from so many different parts of the country. It was memorable to this day.

When it came to deciding on a theme for the NF presentation at the Ideal Home Exhibition in 1972, 'This Green and Pleasant Land?' was chosen as it reflected concern over environmental issues and raised the question of the future of the countryside. The fuel crisis disrupted meetings again in December, when one WI complained: 'there being no heating in Hook-a-Gate School and the use of electric in the Church Hall was not allowed.'

At the dawn of 1974, the national organisation reached a record number of branches, but the ladies of these 9,309 WIs now had to pay an annual subscription of £1 (15p to the NF, 35p to the County Federation and 50p to the WI). The cream of handcrafted items, including seventeen from the Lancashire Federation, was exhibited at the national 'Tomorrow's Heirlooms' Exhibition in London, confirming the WI's ability to preserve traditional crafts and skills. Nowhere was this better demonstrated than by members from West Kent, who deftly embroidered the NF coat of arms, awarded to commemorate their Diamond Jubilee in 1975, onto a tablecloth for use at national meetings. The Queen's Silver Jubilee in 1977 was cause for more festivities, and Hilton WI, in Cambridgeshire, was among those whose celebration reflected their community spirit, for they offered cream teas and improved the environment by cleaning roads and bridleways in the village. The village celebrations that Milton Malsor WI were involved with were far more racy, for a number of members added to the fun by dressing up as 'bunny girls' for their float. Equally busy were WI Sports and Leisure sub-committees with members engaging in activities ranging from bowling matches to tennis tournaments at The Queen's Club, London.

The first of two significant events in the 1980s was the Life and Leisure Exhibition held in 1984, for this was the first time that the WI had put on their very own show at Olympia. Every WI from every federation was involved and Gwen Garner records how the six-day event attracted 55,000 visitors, who purchased tens of thousands of craft items as well as 5,000 jars of preserves. The event was a huge success, and inspired new WIs all over the country as

Bedfordshire Federation members taking part in the Bowls Tournament, 25 September 1978.

well as in London, which had its own federation. The second achievement came at the end of the decade, with their highly successful first appearance at the Chelsea Flower Show. Alongside all the national and royal anniversaries, WIs rarely missed an opportunity to enjoy their own special dates. The Westray branch of the SWRI celebrated its Golden Jubilee in 1980, by producing a recipe book which included local delicacies such as Cuddleston cake and Isle of Rhum gingerbread. In contrast, the ladies of Ashwell WI worked incredibly hard for months before they celebrated their seventieth anniversary in 1988, producing a commemorative quilt that they proudly presented to the village museum. Shugborough Hall was the grand venue for the seventieth anniversary of the Staffordshire Federation in June

Milton Malsor WI ladies dressed up as 'bunny girls' on their float in 1977.

The Staffordshire FWI celebrated their seventieth anniversary at Shugborough in June 1989. The theme was 'A Cavalcade Through the Years', with each WI choosing a theme from the year of their formation.

1989, with each WI choosing a theme from the year of their formation for their pageant, 'Cavalcade Through the Years.'

The WIs greeted 1990, the year of the national seventy-fifth anniversary, in excellent company, for Her Majesty the Queen addressed their AGM at the Royal Albert Hall, the last occasion that the meeting was held there. After that, general meetings were held every three years. *Home and Country* magazine celebrated seventy-five years of publication in 1994. And as the century closed, fame came to the Rylstone and District branch in North Yorkshire, when the members posed for a 'not quite nude' calendar in aid of Leukaemia Research. This was so successful that a star-studded film and stage show, *Calendar Girls*, followed, continuing the charity work into the twenty-first century.

The WI has come a long way since the first organisation was set up in Wales in 1917. No one then would have dreamt that an incumbent Prime Minister would be addressing 6,000 WI ladies at their Triennial General Meeting in Millennium Year, 2000. But this was exactly the scenario, when Tony Blair used the platform in Cardiff on 7 June 2000 for party-political purposes, only to be greeted by the slow handclapping of 6,000 disenchanted members. Less fractious NF celebrations were the wonderful Craft Spectacular at Tatton Park, Cheshire, and the compilation of a Denman College millennium book, while local WIs marked the occasion in their own personal way. Just one example was the Millennium Fund, set up in 1988 by the Bedfordshire Federation, which had reached a staggering sum of £13,169

Edith Turnock, 79, completes the world's first knitted billboard, celebrating the launch of Sky and the Women's Institute's nationwide search to find the ultimate W-Icon, 3 June 2008 in London.

Ashwell WI presents its seventieth-anniversary quilt to the village museum, June 1988.

Rylstone Women's Institute members launch their new calendar for 2004, in the Yorkshire Dales. The Calendar also featured Helen Mirren and Julie Walters, who appeared in the film *Calendar Girls*.

Ladies from Kirkby Malzeard WI, North Yorkshire, collecting litter, *c.* 2002–03.

at the close of 2000, enabling them to donate medical equipment to a number of local hospitals.

The twenty-first century saw new WIs blossoming in the inner cities, attracting much younger women, the comedy drama series 'Jam and Jerusalem' was launched, and at the end of 2006, *Home and Country* was replaced with *WI Life*. In 2009, the magazine underwent a further transformation and Neil Maidment, editor and the first man to hold this post, told the *Guardian*:

> In an effort to move away from the image of it being a 'club for old ladies' the next issue will feature Jazz Holly, a 25-year-old Shoreditch resident and WI member on the cover.

Members were trying their hand at all sorts of activities, including target shooting, darts and gliding lessons, which would not have been dreamt of in 1917. Lobbying became much more sophisticated, with WI ladies actively involving themselves in the debate over environmental issues, prison reform and more. The 'Comforts for Troops' provided by the Suffolk West Federation in 2010 were much appreciated, as they were in 1941, but these grateful recipients were fighting a war in Afghanistan rather than Europe. And mirroring the 1940s, when WI ladies taught children to knit, the NF joined forces with the Crafts Council and the UK Hand Knitting Association to help teach young people to master the art. Jam making was celebrated with the first WI Real Jam Festival, while singing acquired a new status. The early members of Llanfair PG would be astonished to learn that, in 2010, 'The Harmonies', a five-woman band selected from an initial 600 entrants, were

Audrey Elliott showing her fellow WI members how to saw wood at a DIY class organised by B&Q, held at Denman College on 1 March 2010.

Members and guests at Bramley WI Lite's third birthday party had a ball, served by their 'butler in the buff'. The Lite group devolved from the regular WI group to 'take the best bits of traditional WI and give them a makeover'.

signed up by Universal Records. Their first album, 'The Voices of the WI', released in October, does, of course, include a rendition of 'Jerusalem'. Words addressed to the WI by John Bercow, the Speaker of the House of Commons, by video link on 2 June 2010, ring very true:

> ... there are aspects about the way that your institution has changed in the past few decades which I think set an example to us at Westminster .... The reality is that we are both complicated organisations that have to change with the times to retain relevance.

This is a path that the WI will no doubt follow for decades to come.

FURTHER READING

BOOKS

Garner, Gwen. *Extra Ordinary Women. A History of the Women's Institutes.* WI Books Ltd., 1995.

Gibson, Lorna. *Beyond Jerusalem: Music in the Women's Institute, 1919–1969.* Ashgate, Aldershot, 2008.

Goodenough, Simon, *Jam and Jerusalem, A Pictorial History of the Women's Institute.* Collins, 1977.

Jenkins, Inez. *The History of the Women's Institute Movement of England and Wales.* Charles Batey, Oxford, 1953.

Kitchen, Penny. *For Home and Country.* Ebury Press, 1990.

McCall, Cicely. *Women's Institutes.* Collins, 1943. Britain in Pictures Series No. 61.

Scott, John William Robertson. *The Story of the Women's Institute Movement in England & Wales & Scotland.* Village Press, Kingham, Oxfordshire, 1925.

Stamper, Anne. *Rooms off the Corridor. Education in the WI and 50 Years of Denman College 1948–1998.* WI Books, 1998.

WEBSITES

The official NFWI website has a wealth of information about the organization. www.thewi.org.uk

The SWRI has its own website, www.swri.org.uk, as does the Federation of Women's Institutes of Northern Ireland. www.wini.org.uk

The papers of the NFWI for 1915–2005 (5FWI) can be found at The Women's Library, London Metropolitan University

A search of the National Register of Archives reveals the existence of documents in record offices relating to several hundred local Women's Institutes all over England. A search of the Archives' Wales catalogue provides similar information about Welsh WIs, as does a search of the Scottish Archive Network for local Scottish Women's Rural Institutes. A search of the eCatalogue of the Public Record Office of Northern Ireland reveals the existence of documents in record offices relating to Women's Institutes in Northern Ireland.

INDEX